Chapter 1: The Wealthy vs. the Wannabe Wealthy

The concept of wealth is often misunderstood. Many people assume that high-income earners are automatically wealthy, but *The Millionaire Next Door* by Thomas J. Stanley reveals a different reality. True wealth is not about how much money you make—it's about how much you keep, grow, and manage wisely.

In this chapter, we'll explore the fundamental differences between real millionaires and those who only appear wealthy. Through interactive activities, you'll assess your financial habits, learn to recognize the behaviors of true millionaires, and analyze real-life scenarios to determine who is on the path to lasting wealth.

1. Quiz: Are You a Future Millionaire?

Do you have the mindset and habits of a future millionaire? Take this quiz to find out. Answer each question honestly and keep track of your responses.

Instructions:

For each question, choose the answer that best describes your current habits. At the end of the quiz, use the scoring guide to see where you stand on the path to financial independence.

Question 1: How do you approach budgeting?

A) I create and follow a detailed budget each month.

B) I have a rough idea of my expenses but don't track everything.

C) I spend as needed and figure out the rest later.

Question 2: What do you do with unexpected income (bonuses, tax refunds, gifts)?

A) Save or invest most of it.

B) Save a portion, but also treat myself.

C) Spend it on something fun—I earned it!

Question 3: When it comes to cars, which best describes your approach?

A) I drive a reliable, modestly priced car and keep it for many years.

B) I lease or finance a new car every few years.

C) I prefer luxury or high-performance cars, even if it means a high monthly payment.

Question 4: How much of your income do you save or invest each year?

A) At least 20% or more.

B) Between 10-20%.

C) Less than 10% or none.

Question 5: Do you track your net worth (assets minus liabilities)?

A) Yes, I update it regularly and use it to guide financial decisions.

B) I have a general idea but don't track it closely.

C) I don't know my net worth.

Question 6: What's your approach to clothing and luxury items?

A) I focus on quality over brand names and buy only what I need.

B) I mix high-end and budget-friendly items.

C) I prefer designer brands and enjoy keeping up with the latest trends.

Question 7: How do you handle debt?

A) I avoid unnecessary debt and pay off balances quickly.

B) I have some debt but manage it responsibly.

C) I use credit for major purchases and carry balances regularly.

Scoring Guide:

- **Mostly A's:** You have the mindset and habits of a future millionaire. You prioritize savings, live below your means, and focus on long-term financial security.

- **Mostly B's:** You're on the right track but may need to refine some habits to build wealth more effectively. Consider increasing savings and reducing lifestyle inflation.

- **Mostly C's:** Your financial habits could prevent you from becoming truly wealthy. Focus on budgeting, reducing unnecessary spending, and investing for the future.

2. Spot the Difference: Millionaire vs. High-Income Spender

Many people assume that wealth and high income are the same, but they are not. A person can earn a six-figure salary and still be broke, while another person making far less can be a millionaire. Let's compare the behaviors of true millionaires with those of high-income spenders.

Activity: Who's Who?

Below are descriptions of two individuals. Read carefully and determine which one is the true millionaire and which one is the high-income spender.

Person A:

- Earns $250,000 per year.

- Lives in a large home with a mortgage that takes up 40% of their income.

- Drives a brand-new luxury car with high monthly payments.

- Rarely saves more than 5% of their income.

- Uses credit cards frequently and carries a balance.

Person B:

- Earns $80,000 per year.

- Lives in a modest home with a mortgage that is less than 15% of their income.

- Drives a reliable car that is fully paid off.

- Saves and invests 25% of their income consistently.

- Avoids credit card debt and pays off balances each month.

Who is the real millionaire?

If you guessed **Person B**, you're correct! Despite earning far less than Person A, they have wealth-building habits—low expenses, a strong savings rate, and minimal debt. Person A, despite their high income, is trapped in a cycle of spending and debt, making it difficult to accumulate lasting wealth.

Key Takeaways:

- **Wealth is what you keep, not what you earn.**

- **Millionaires live below their means, while high-income spenders focus on appearances.**

- **Financial freedom comes from disciplined saving and investing, not just a high paycheck.**

3. Case Study Analysis: Millionaire or Not?

In this section, we'll look at three fictional case studies. Your task is to analyze their financial behaviors and decide whether they are likely to become wealthy or struggle financially.

Case Study #1: Lisa – The Frugal Investor

Lisa is a middle school teacher earning $60,000 per year. She saves 30% of her income, invests in low-cost index funds, and drives a 10-year-old Toyota.

She lives in a small house, avoids credit card debt, and buys quality items only when necessary.

Question:

Is Lisa on the path to becoming a millionaire? **Why or why not?**

Case Study #2: Mark – The Flashy Entrepreneur

Mark owns a business and makes $400,000 a year. He lives in a luxury condo, frequently travels first-class, and drives a new sports car. He reinvests some of his income into his business but rarely saves or invests outside of it. He has a large mortgage and significant credit card debt.

Question:

Will Mark achieve lasting wealth? **Why or why not?**

Case Study #3: Sarah and Tom – The Responsible Couple

Sarah and Tom both work government jobs, earning a combined $120,000 per year. They max out their retirement accounts, live in a modest home, and drive older cars. They prioritize experiences over material things and have a net worth of $1.2 million despite their moderate income.

Question:

How did Sarah and Tom achieve millionaire status? **What can others learn from them?**

Reflection Questions:

1. Which financial behaviors in these case studies contribute to long-term wealth?

2. What are some common mistakes that prevent people from becoming millionaires?

3. Based on these case studies, what changes can you make to improve your financial future?

Final Thoughts

The first step to becoming a millionaire is understanding the difference between true wealth and the illusion of wealth. Many people who look rich are actually drowning in debt, while many millionaires live modest lives and quietly build financial security.

By taking this chapter's quiz, identifying key millionaire behaviors, and analyzing case studies, you can start applying these lessons to your own life. The path to financial independence isn't about luck or a high income—it's about smart money management, disciplined savings, and long-term investing.

Are you ready to start thinking and acting like a millionaire next door?

Chapter 2: Living Below Your Means

One of the most important lessons from *The Millionaire Next Door* is that wealthy people don't necessarily earn the most—they spend the least relative to their income. Many millionaires live well below their means, prioritizing savings, investments, and financial security over flashy lifestyles. This chapter will help you adopt the mindset and habits of real millionaires by focusing on budgeting, tracking your spending, and making smart financial choices.

By completing the activities in this chapter, you'll learn how to budget like a millionaire, monitor your spending habits, and make better financial decisions in real-life scenarios.

1. Budget Challenge: The Millionaire's Way

Millionaires don't rely on luck—they create a financial plan and stick to it. A well-structured budget is the foundation of financial success, allowing you to control your money instead of letting it control you. In this section, you'll build a budget using the same principles that self-made millionaires follow.

The Millionaire Budget Formula

Most self-made millionaires follow a simple but powerful budgeting strategy:

- **50% Needs (Housing, Utilities, Food, Insurance, Transportation)**

- **30% Savings & Investments (Retirement, Emergency Fund, Stocks, Real Estate, Business Growth)**

- **20% Wants (Entertainment, Dining Out, Shopping, Travel, Hobbies)**

This approach ensures that wealth-building takes priority over lifestyle inflation. Now, let's create your own millionaire-style budget.

Activity: Your Millionaire Budget Worksheet

Step 1: Calculate Your Monthly Income

Write down your total after-tax income:

💰 **Monthly Income: $_____**

Step 2: Allocate Your Expenses

Fill in the following budget categories based on your income.

- **🏠 Needs (50%)**

  - Rent/Mortgage: $_____

  - Utilities (Electricity, Water, Internet, etc.): $_____

  - Groceries: $_____

  - Insurance (Health, Car, Home): $_____

  - Transportation (Gas, Public Transit, Car Payment): $_____

  - Other Essentials: $_____

  - **Total Needs:** $_____

- **💰 Savings & Investments (30%)**

  - Emergency Fund Contribution: $_____

  - Retirement Accounts (401k, IRA, etc.): $_____

  - Stock/Index Fund Investments: $_____

- Real Estate/Other Investments: $_____

- Debt Repayment (if applicable): $_____

- **Total Savings & Investments: $_____**

- 🎊 **Wants (20%)**

  - Dining Out & Entertainment: $_____

  - Shopping: $_____

  - Travel & Hobbies: $_____

  - Subscriptions & Other Discretionary Spending: $_____

  - **Total Wants: $_____**

Step 3: Compare Your Budget to the Millionaire Formula

- Are you saving and investing at least **30%** of your income?

- Are your "wants" staying within **20%** of your income?

- Do your "needs" stay at **50%** or less?

If your current budget doesn't align with these targets, identify areas where you can cut back. Millionaires focus on controlling expenses so they can invest more for financial freedom.

2. Spending Habits Tracker

Most people don't realize how much they spend until they track it. Millionaires are mindful spenders—they analyze where their money goes and eliminate unnecessary expenses. This section will help you develop that same habit.

Activity: The 7-Day Spending Challenge

For the next **7 days**, write down **everything** you spend money on. At the end of the week, compare your habits to millionaire-like spending patterns.

Day,Category,Amount Spent,Was It Necessary? (Yes/No),Could I Have Saved This Money? (Yes/No)

Monday,Groceries,$_____,Yes/No,Yes/No

Monday,Coffee Shop,$_____,Yes/No,Yes/No

Monday,Online Shopping,$_____,Yes/No,Yes/No

…,…,…,…,…

Sunday,Streaming Subscription,$_____,Yes/No,Yes/No

Category,Millionaires' Habits,Average Person's Habits

Housing,Buy modest homes and live below their means,Buy expensive homes, often stretching their budgets

Cars,Drive used or modest vehicles, rarely lease,Finance or lease luxury cars

Eating Out,Cook at home, limit restaurant spending,Frequently eat out and order takeout

Shopping,Buy quality essentials, avoid trendy splurges,Spend impulsively on fashion and gadgets

Vacations,Use travel rewards, plan budget-friendly trips,Take luxury vacations on credit

Debt Management,Avoid debt and pay off balances quickly,Carry credit card debt and pay high interest

3. Scenario Game: What Would a Millionaire Do?

Millionaires make financial choices that prioritize long-term wealth. In this game, you'll be presented with different situations. Your job is to choose the best financial decision and learn why it leads to wealth.

Scenario 1: The Car Purchase

You need a new vehicle. You have the following options:

A) Buy a reliable used car with cash ($12,000).
B) Lease a brand-new luxury SUV with a $700 monthly payment.
C) Finance a new mid-range car with a $400 monthly payment.

Best Millionaire Choice: A) Buy a used car with cash.

💡 **Why?** Millionaires avoid car loans because vehicles rapidly depreciate. A reliable used car keeps costs low and allows more money for investing.

Scenario 2: The Unexpected Bonus

You receive a $5,000 year-end bonus. What do you do?

A) Invest the full amount in index funds.
B) Take a vacation and buy new furniture.
C) Put half into savings and spend the rest.

Best Millionaire Choice: A) Invest the full amount.
💡 **Why?** Millionaires use unexpected income to grow their wealth instead of increasing their lifestyle expenses.

Scenario 3: Housing Decision

You're considering buying a home. What's the best approach?

A) Purchase a modest home well below your budget.

B) Buy a big house with a mortgage that takes up 40% of your income.

C) Rent for now and spend more on lifestyle.

Best Millionaire Choice: A) Buy a modest home well below your budget.

💡 **Why?** Millionaires prioritize affordability so they can invest more. A lower mortgage means financial flexibility and security.

Scenario 4: Job Offer with a Pay Raise

You get a new job with a 20% salary increase. What's your next move?

A) Keep your expenses the same and invest the extra income.

B) Upgrade to a larger house and new car.

C) Increase spending a little but save some as well.

Best Millionaire Choice: A) Keep expenses the same and invest the extra income.

💡 **Why?** Avoiding lifestyle inflation is key to long-term wealth. Millionaires save and invest pay raises instead of upgrading their lifestyle.

Final Thoughts

Living below your means is the secret to financial freedom. Millionaires focus on **saving, investing, and minimizing unnecessary expenses** rather than appearing rich.

By completing the **Budget Challenge, Spending Tracker, and Scenario Game**, you've taken major steps toward adopting the millionaire mindset. Your next step? **Apply these habits consistently!**

Key Takeaways:

✓ Budget with a focus on **saving and investing** (30% of income).

✓ Track spending and eliminate **wasteful expenses**.

✓ Make smart financial decisions based on **long-term wealth-building**.

Are you ready to start living like a millionaire next door?

Chapter 3: Financial Independence Over Status

One of the biggest financial myths is that wealthy people drive the most expensive cars, live in the biggest houses, and wear designer brands. But *The Millionaire Next Door* by Thomas J. Stanley reveals a surprising truth: most millionaires don't care about status symbols. Instead, they prioritize **financial**

independence—the ability to live life on their terms, without worrying about debt or financial insecurity.

This chapter will help you shift your mindset from chasing status to building lasting wealth. Through interactive activities, you'll see how real millionaires manage their money, calculate the hidden costs of lifestyle inflation, and commit to a future of financial independence.

1. Who's Driving What?

Most people assume that millionaires drive luxury cars like Ferraris, BMWs, or Bentleys. In reality, self-made millionaires often drive practical, modest vehicles. Why? Because they focus on **financial freedom over flashy status symbols**.

Studies show that the most common car brands driven by millionaires are **Toyota, Honda, and Ford**—not Lamborghini or Rolls-Royce. These wealthy individuals understand that cars **depreciate in value**, making them a poor investment. Instead of spending money on expensive vehicles, they invest their wealth in assets that grow over time, like stocks, real estate, and businesses.

Activity: Match the Car to the Millionaire

Below are three people with different financial habits. Can you match them to the car they're most likely to drive?

Person A: The Status Seeker

- Earns $250,000 per year but spends most of it.

- Finances a new luxury car every 3 years.

- Carries credit card debt and has little savings.

- Wants to appear successful, even if it means living paycheck to paycheck.

Person B: The Millionaire Next Door

- Earns $80,000 per year but has a net worth of over $1 million.

- Drives a used Toyota Camry with no car payment.

- Saves 30% of income and invests consistently.

- Values financial security over impressing others.

Person C: The High-Income Saver

- Earns $150,000 per year and is working toward financial independence.

- Bought a reliable Honda Accord with cash.

- Prioritizes maxing out retirement accounts.

- Plans to retire early by keeping expenses low.

Car Options:

1. 🚗 **Brand-New Mercedes-Benz (Financed, $900/month payment)**

2. 🚙 **5-Year-Old Toyota Camry (Paid in full, no payments)**

3. ☐ **Certified Pre-Owned Honda Accord (Paid in cash, low maintenance costs)**

Answer Key:

- **Person A → 🚗 Brand-New Mercedes-Benz**

- **Person B → 🚙 5-Year-Old Toyota Camry**

- **Person C → □ Certified Pre-Owned Honda Accord**

Reflection:

1. **Which person is on the best path to financial independence? Why?**

2. **Would you rather drive a flashy car and struggle financially or have financial freedom with a modest car?**

3. **How much could you save in 10 years by avoiding expensive car payments?**

☞ **Lesson:** Millionaires don't waste money on depreciating assets like luxury cars. They **buy practical vehicles, keep them for years, and invest the savings**.

2. The True Cost of Lifestyle Inflation

Lifestyle inflation is one of the biggest obstacles to financial independence. When people earn more money, they tend to **increase their spending** instead of saving or investing. This keeps them trapped in a cycle of working just to afford an expensive lifestyle.

How Lifestyle Inflation Works

Imagine two people, **Alex** and **Jordan**, both starting out with a $50,000 salary. Over time, they receive raises—but they handle their money very differently

Year,Alex's Salary,Alex's Spending,Alex's Savings,Jordan's Salary,Jordan's Spending,Jordan's Savings
Year 1,$50,000,$40,000,$10,000,$50,000,$40,000,$10,000

Year

5,$70,000,$42,000,$28,000,$70,000,$65,000,$5,000

Year

10,$100,000,$45,000,$55,000,$100,000,$95,000,$5,
000

Key Observations:

- **Alex kept expenses low**, even as income grew, allowing for massive savings.

- **Jordan increased spending** every time they got a raise, leaving little for savings.

- After 10 years, **Alex has $55,000 saved** while **Jordan has only $5,000**.

☞ **Lesson:** If you increase your spending every time you earn more, you'll never build wealth. Millionaires resist lifestyle inflation and focus on **financial security first**.

Activity: Calculate the Cost of Lifestyle Inflation

Think about a recent pay raise or bonus. If you had saved or invested that money instead of spending it, how much would it have grown?

1. **Last pay raise/bonus amount: $_____**

2. **How much did you save? $_____**

3. **How much did you spend? $_____**

4. **If you invested the full amount for 10 years at 7% growth, how much would it be worth?**

Use this rule of thumb:

- $1,000 invested at 7% annual growth = **$1,967 in 10 years**

- $5,000 invested at 7% annual growth = **$9,835 in 10 years**

- $10,000 invested at 7% annual growth = **$19,672 in 10 years**

Reflection:

- Did lifestyle inflation take away potential investments?

- How can you resist lifestyle inflation in the future?

- What changes can you make today to prioritize **wealth over status**?

3. Letter to Your Future Self

Financial independence isn't just about numbers—it's about setting clear goals and committing to them. Writing a letter to your future self can help you **stay focused on your financial journey**.

Activity: Write a Letter to Your Future Self

Imagine it's **10 years from now**. You've followed the principles of financial independence, avoided lifestyle inflation, and built real wealth. Write a letter from your future self to the present you.

Use these prompts to guide your letter:

1. **What does your financial life look like in 10 years?**

   - How much have you saved and invested?

   - Are you debt-free?

   - Have you reached financial independence?

2. **What sacrifices did you make to get there?**

- Did you avoid unnecessary spending?

- Did you resist upgrading your lifestyle?

- How did you stay disciplined?

3. **What advice would your future self give to the present you?**

- How can you stay focused on your goals?

- What financial mistakes should you avoid?

- What mindset shifts are necessary to build wealth?

Example Letter to Your Future Self

Dear Future Me,

Right now, I'm working hard to build financial independence. I know it's not always easy—I see others buying expensive cars, taking luxury vacations, and living beyond their means. But I also know that true wealth isn't about status symbols; it's about freedom.

I'm making smart choices today:

- I'm living below my means.

- I'm saving and investing at least 30% of my income.

- I'm avoiding unnecessary debt and staying focused on long-term goals.

Future me, I hope you're reading this from a place of **financial freedom**. I hope you own your time, have no financial stress, and can live life on your terms.

No matter what challenges come, **remember why you started**. Stay disciplined, stay frugal, and always put financial independence over status.

Sincerely,

Your Past Self

Final Thoughts

Many people fall into the trap of **chasing status instead of building real wealth**. But true financial independence comes from smart financial habits—not flashy purchases.

Key Takeaways:

✅ **Millionaires drive modest cars and avoid debt.**

✅ **Lifestyle inflation can keep you broke—even with a high income.**

✅ **Committing to financial independence today will give you freedom in the future.**

Are you ready to choose financial freedom over status? **Start making the right money choices today!**

Chapter 4: Investing and Growing Wealth

One of the most important lessons from *The Millionaire Next Door* is that **wealth isn't built by earning a high salary alone—it's built through smart investing**. Millionaires don't just save their money; they put it to work through investments that grow over time.

This chapter will help you understand key investment terms, explore the incredible power of

compound interest, and create your own investment plan. By the end, you'll have a roadmap for growing your wealth like a true millionaire next door.

1. Investment Word Search

Before diving into investment strategies, let's familiarize ourselves with some key terms. These words are essential to understanding how millionaires grow their wealth.

Key Investment Terms

- **Compound Interest** – Interest earned on both the initial investment and the accumulated interest over time.

- **Diversification** – Spreading investments across different assets to reduce risk.

- **Index Fund** – A type of mutual fund or ETF that tracks a stock market index like the S&P 500.

- **Asset Allocation** – The strategy of dividing investments among different categories (stocks, bonds, real estate, etc.).

- **Stock Market** – A place where investors buy and sell shares of companies.

- **Risk Tolerance** – An investor's ability to handle losses in the market.

- **Inflation** – The gradual increase in prices over time, reducing the purchasing power of money.

- **Retirement Fund** – Accounts like 401(k)s or IRAs used for long-term wealth building.

Activity: Investment Word Search

Find and circle the following words in the word search puzzle below:

🔍 Compound Interest | Diversification | Index Fund | Stock Market | Asset Allocation | Risk Tolerance | Inflation | Retirement Fund

(You can create this puzzle online using a word search generator.)

Reflection Questions:

1. Were any of these terms new to you?

2. How do you think these concepts help millionaires grow wealth?

3. Which investment terms do you want to learn more about?

☞ **Lesson:** Understanding investment basics is the first step to financial success. Now, let's see how **compound interest** can make your money grow!

2. Millionaire Math: The Power of Compound Interest

What is Compound Interest?

Compound interest is **the secret weapon of wealth-building**. It allows your money to grow exponentially over time. Instead of just earning interest on your initial deposit, you also earn interest on your **previous interest**.

The Rule of 72

Want to know how fast your money will double? Use this simple formula:

72 ÷ Annual Return Rate = Years to Double Your Money

For example:

- If you invest in a fund that earns **8% per year**, your money will double in **9 years (72 ÷ 8 = 9)**.

- If you earn **10% per year**, your money doubles in **7.2 years (72 ÷ 10 = 7.2)**.

Activity: How Much Will Your Money Grow?

Let's see how different investment amounts grow over time using compound interest.

Scenario: You invest a certain amount in the stock market and leave it for **30 years** at a **10% average annual return** (the historical return of the S&P 500)

Starting Investment,10 Years,20 Years,30 Years
$1,000,$2,593,$6,727,$17,449

$5,000,$12,963,$33,637,$87,197

$10,000,$25,927,$67,275,$174,494

$50,000,$129,637,$336,375,$872,470

Reflection Questions:

1. How much could you grow your money by investing early?

2. What happens if you delay investing by 10 years?

3. How does compound interest compare to just saving money in a bank?

☞ **Lesson:** The earlier you start investing, the **more powerful compound interest becomes**. Even small investments can turn into **huge amounts** over time.

3. Build Your Own Investment Plan

Now that you understand the power of investing, it's time to create your own **investment strategy**. Millionaires **don't leave their money sitting in a savings account**—they make a plan and stick to it.

Step 1: Set Your Investment Goals

Answer these questions to define your investment strategy:

1. **What are you investing for?** (Retirement, financial independence, buying a home, etc.)

2. **How long do you plan to invest?** (Short-term: 1-5 years, Medium-term: 5-15 years, Long-term: 15+ years)

3. **How much can you invest each month?** ($50, $100, $500, more?)

Step 2: Choose Your Investment Vehicles

Millionaires use different **types of investments** to grow their wealth. Choose which ones fit your goals Investment Type,Risk Level,Potential Return,Good for Beginners?

Index Funds (S&P 500, Total Market Funds),Medium,8-10% per year,✓ Yes

Individual Stocks,High,Varies,✗ No (Too risky)

Real Estate (Rental Properties, REITs),Medium,5-12% per year,✓ Yes

Bonds (Treasury, Corporate, Municipal),Low,2-5% per year,✓ Yes

Crypto & Alternative Investments,Very High,10-100% (or losses),✗ No (Very risky)

Millionaire Strategy: Most self-made millionaires invest **primarily in index funds and real estate** because they offer strong growth with low risk.

Step 3: Create Your Investment Plan

Fill in the blanks to create a personalized plan:

1. **My main investment goal is:**

   _____

2. **I will invest $_____ per month.**

3. **My investment mix will be:**

   - ___% Index Funds

   - ___% Real Estate

   - ___% Bonds

   - ___% Other Investments

4. **I will review my investments every:**
(month, 6 months, year)

Step 4: Automate and Stay Consistent

Millionaires don't **try to time the market**—they **invest consistently** no matter what the market is doing. The best way to do this? **Automate your investments.**

Ways to automate your investing:

✓ Set up **automatic contributions** to a brokerage account.

✓ Use a **401(k) or IRA** for tax-advantaged investing.

✓ Choose **low-cost index funds** that require minimal management.

☞ **Lesson: Consistency is the key to wealth.** Even small amounts invested **every month** can lead to financial freedom.

Final Thoughts: Start Investing Today!

Most millionaires don't get rich overnight—they build wealth **slowly and consistently through smart investing**. The earlier you start, the more **compound interest** can work in your favor.

Key Takeaways:

✅ Investing early and consistently leads to wealth.

✅ Index funds and real estate are the top choices for millionaires.

✅ Avoid risky, get-rich-quick investments.

✅ Automate your investments to stay disciplined.

Your Next Steps:

📌 **Open an investment account** (Vanguard, Fidelity, Charles Schwab, etc.).

📌 **Invest in an index fund** (S&P 500 or Total Market Fund).

📌 **Set up automatic contributions** so you invest every month.

🚀 **The best time to start investing was yesterday. The second-best time is NOW.** What will you do today to start building wealth like a millionaire?

Chapter 5: Teaching the Next Generation

One of the most important responsibilities of financially successful individuals is **passing down good money habits to the next generation**. The millionaire next door isn't just focused on personal wealth—they teach their children how to **manage money wisely** so that financial success continues for generations.

Unfortunately, many parents fail to teach their children about money, leading to financial struggles later in life. By teaching kids smart financial habits early, parents can help them develop a **strong foundation for wealth-building and financial independence**.

This chapter will explore **practical ways to teach children about money**, compare different allowance strategies, and help families create a **financial vision board** to set long-term goals.

1. Millionaire Money Lessons for Kids

Raising financially responsible children starts with **teaching smart money habits from a young age**. Many self-made millionaires learned about **saving,**

investing, and avoiding debt early in life, which gave them a head start in wealth-building.

Here's a checklist of **simple but powerful financial lessons** parents can teach their children:

✅ Smart Spending and Saving Habits

• **Teach delayed gratification** – Kids should learn to wait before making purchases instead of spending impulsively.

• **Encourage saving a percentage of all money received** – Whether from gifts, chores, or jobs, children should save at least 20-50%.

• **Use a clear jar or savings app** – Seeing money grow motivates kids to keep saving.

• **Set savings goals** – If a child wants a toy or game, help them set a goal and track progress.

✅ The Value of Work and Earning Money

- **Teach kids that money is earned, not given** – Encourage them to work for money through age-appropriate chores, pet-sitting, or small entrepreneurial ventures.

- **Create opportunities for kids to earn money** – Lemonade stands, selling crafts, or mowing lawns are great ways to introduce entrepreneurship.

- **Teach kids about taxes and deductions** – If they earn money, explain how some will go to savings, giving, and spending.

✅ Investing and Growing Wealth

- **Explain how money can grow through investing** – Show them how $10 invested today can turn into much more over time.

- **Use simple compound interest examples** – If they invest $100 at 10% interest, it will become $259 in 10 years.

- **Open a custodial investment account** – Let kids see how investments grow over time.

✅ Avoiding Debt and Making Smart Financial Choices

- **Teach kids to avoid debt early** – Explain why borrowing money (except for smart investments like a house) can lead to financial stress.

- **Lead by example** – If kids see parents budgeting and making smart money choices, they will follow.

Activity: Financial Habit Tracker for Kids

Create a simple chart where kids can check off financial habits they practice daily or weekly, such as:

✓ Saved a portion of my money

✓ Waited before buying something

✓ Earned money by doing a job

✓ Asked about the price before spending

✓ Learned something new about money

Reflection:

- Which of these lessons do you already teach your kids?

- What new lessons can you start teaching today?

☞ **Lesson:** Millionaires **teach their kids about money early**, so they don't have to learn financial lessons the hard way later in life.

2. Allowance vs. Earnings: What's the Best Strategy?

One of the biggest questions parents face is **how to give their children money**—should it be an **allowance** or should kids **earn their own money**? There are pros and cons to both approaches.

Option 1: Giving a Regular Allowance

An allowance means giving kids a set amount of money each week or month, usually based on age.

✅ **Pros:**

- Teaches kids how to budget.

- Helps them understand saving vs. spending.

- Gives them responsibility for making money decisions.

✗ Cons:

- Kids may expect money without working for it.

- Doesn't teach the true value of earning money.

- Can create entitlement if not managed properly.

Option 2: Making Kids Earn Their Own Money

Instead of receiving money automatically, kids can **earn money through chores, small jobs, or business ventures**.

✅ **Pros:**

- Teaches kids that money is **earned, not given**.

- Builds a strong work ethic.

- Helps kids develop creativity and problem-solving skills.

❌ **Cons:**

- May require extra effort from parents to set up earning opportunities.

- Kids may resist working if they are used to receiving an allowance.

Option 3: A Hybrid Approach

Many financial experts recommend a **hybrid system** where kids receive a small basic allowance for needs but must **earn extra money through work**.

💡 **Example System:**

- **Base Allowance:** $5 per week for basic needs (learning to budget).

- **Earnings:** Kids can do extra chores or jobs to **earn more money** beyond the base allowance.

- **Savings Requirement:** 50% of all money earned must go into a savings or investment account.

Activity: Pros and Cons List

Ask your kids to list the advantages and disadvantages of getting an allowance vs. earning money.

Reflection Questions:

• If you had to choose, would you rather get an allowance or earn money? Why?

• What kind of work would you be willing to do to earn money?

• How would you handle money differently if you had to earn it yourself?

☞ **Lesson:** Millionaire parents teach their kids **the value of hard work and earning money**, rather than just giving them handouts.

3. Family Financial Vision Board

A great way to **motivate the entire family** to focus on financial goals is to create a **Family Financial Vision Board**.

What is a Vision Board?

A vision board is a **visual representation of goals** using pictures, quotes, and charts. This activity helps families clarify their financial priorities and stay focused on achieving them.

Step 1: Gather Your Supplies

You'll need:

✓ A large poster board or digital vision board app

✓ Magazines, printed images, or drawings

✓ Scissors, glue, markers, and stickers

Step 2: Define Your Family's Financial Goals

As a family, discuss and decide on financial goals.
Some ideas include:

- **Saving for a vacation**

- **Paying off debt**

- **Investing for the future**

- **Starting a business**

- **Buying a home**

- **Donating to charity**

Step 3: Find Visual Representations

Cut out or print pictures that represent each goal.
For example:

- A **beach** for a vacation fund

- A **house** for homeownership goals

- A **piggy bank** for savings goals

Step 4: Display and Review the Vision Board

Put the vision board in a visible place (kitchen, living room, or digital version on a phone or tablet). **Review it regularly** to track progress.

Activity: Family Vision Board Questions

1. What are the top three financial goals for our family?

2. How can each family member contribute to these goals?

3. What sacrifices might we need to make to reach these goals?

☞ **Lesson: A vision board makes financial goals real** and helps families stay focused on achieving them together.

Final Thoughts: Passing Down Wealth-Building Habits

Teaching the next generation about money is one of the greatest gifts parents can give. **Financial education should start early**, focusing on smart money habits, the value of work, and long-term goals.

Key Takeaways:

✅ **Teach kids about earning, saving, and investing early.**
✅ **Encourage kids to work for their money rather than expecting handouts.**

✓ Use tools like a financial vision board to set and track family goals.

Your Next Steps:

📌 Start teaching your kids money lessons today.

📌 Decide on an allowance or earning system that fits your family.

📌 Create a financial vision board as a family project.

🚀 The habits you teach today will shape your children's financial future. Will you help them build wealth the right way?

Printed in Dunstable, United Kingdom